Dig Up Your Hidden Family History

by

Debra Trigg Conrad

Dig Up Your Hidden Family History

DEDICATION

This book is dedicated to my amazing mother and father who taught me to love history, explore the beauty of our countryside and appreciate all the discoveries, inventions and priceless treasures found along the journey; and also to my sister, Linda, and niece, Patricia, who have shared all the joys and frustrations in our own genealogy.

Thanks for all your support and encouragement through the years and I love you all!

Dig Up Your Hidden Family History

ABOUT THE AUTHOR

Debra Trigg Conrad is a respected marketing and advertising specialist, business owner, entrepreneur, mentor, and business coach. She has also logged over 12 years of experience as a professional artist and painting instructor.

But perhaps the moniker she's most proud of is being an 'untraditional' western historian, having authored Yuma Mesa Homesteaders 1948 and 1952 by personal request of the Yuma Historical Society.

Debra comes by her interest in western history and genealogy naturally, having traveled extensively through western North America growing up.

Her personal experience researching unusual resources, both online and offline, have given her a rare glimpse into additional ways to unearth sometimes the most hidden bits of family history.

Debra's love of seeing history preserved, combined with her experience on behalf of the Yuma Historical Society, has led her to provide this easy-to-follow treasure map of new resources.

Debra resides in her hometown of Yuma, Arizona with her husband and dogs, and she enjoys frequent travels to Mexico and Italy.

TABLE OF CONTENTS

Prologue

Dedication

The Author Page

*"Everyday of your life is a page of your history...
We are always the same age inside."* ~ *Gertrude Stein*

1 DISCOVERING YOUR ANCESTRY OR GENEALOGY OFFLINE

Examining our own ancestry is far more than just an interesting topic. It can be fascinating and exciting, - or it can be disappointing and shocking. Usually, one finds it to be a quirky combination of both.

As you study your ancestors, you begin to see yourself better, more clearly, because these people gave you your existence. Everything that sets you apart from other human beings, your character, your likes, your dislikes, were derived from your ancestors, the same ones you are trying to discover now.

Now days, more and more people are finding themselves drawn by the mystic of their ancestors. Who were they? What kind of lives did they live? Are there any jailbirds hidden among the more upstanding citizens?

People world-wide are continually inquiring into their ancestors, and the questions are usually the same. After getting past the initial discovery, we tend to investigate deeper in hopes to answer questions like, When did they arrive in America? What part of the country did they settle? Did they run a mercantile, have an education or were circuit riding ministers? Finally the questions are funneled down to - Who were their children? and What became of them?

Tracking one's ancestry is a charmed task for certain but to undertake the journey is neither easy nor safe. After all, there is no telling who you will meet along the way, or what you will find out that has been hidden for years. Hopefully, by the time you have filled in the gaps in your historical family, you will also have a better view of who "You" are today.

Most ancestry seekers enjoy the thrill of the investigation and the game connected with the search. They soon come to realize finding one's ancestors and meeting them through records and history cannot produce its greatest enjoyment unless it is done by the family member. Hiring someone else to conduct the research is not nearly as fulfilling and exciting. Like many of the pleasures of life, ancestor hunting must be experienced firsthand for the greatest joy and charm.

Conducting family research is usually a major gamble. You can completely waste days, weeks, even months - with nothing to show for it. Or you can have multiple generations of data fall easily into your lap on one productive afternoon of research.

The Reason For This Guide -

The reason for this simple guide is to help the family genealogist find and awaken the documentation that has been hidden away for years.

"The life given us by nature is short. But the memory of a well-spent life is eternal." ~Cicero

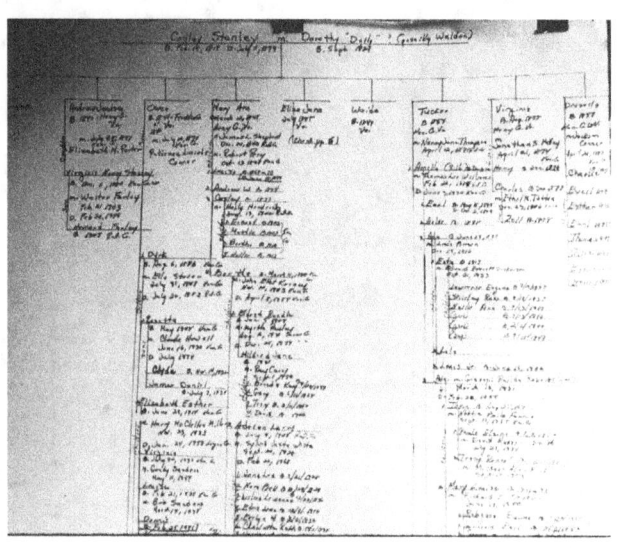

2 EVERY FAMILY HISTORY HAS TWO BRANCHES

The study of the history of a family is best divided into two areas, for better understanding.

The ANCESTRAL viewpoint is the history of a portion of many families converging in one person in the present, usually the seeker himself. I like to equate the ANCESTRAL line as a funnel with the big opening at the top, then funneling down to a small opening at the bottom (the seeker usually).

The GENEALOGICAL viewpoint is the history of many families diverging from one ancestor at some distant point of time. Conversely, the GENEALOGICAL line has the funnel upside down, with the small point top (beginning with the patriarchal ancestor), then growing as it comes down to the bottom to describe the spreading out of a family tree.

It doesn't take any special training or preparation to be successful in researching your ANCESTRAL line.

It just takes tenacity and a tireless will, as it can often take years and years to achieve the best results.

The GENEALOGICAL line requires more training and skill if it is to be successful. However, the layman shouldn't hesitate to take on such an undertaking. With doing comes confidence and the ability will grow simultaneously, which usually presents a creditable piece of family history work.. Insert chapter one text here. Insert chapter one text here.

Ancestral versus Genealogical – Do You Know There Is A Difference? -

These are specific terms and care should be taken to understand the difference in order to achieve the best results. An Ancestral Chart is a picture or diagram of a descendant and his ancestors. It is the framework or skeleton on which a Family History is built. It may be arranged in any one of a multitude of ways, sometimes resembling an open fan, but more often shown by a plain diagram on one or more sheets of paper ruled for the purpose and indicating the multiplication of lines necessary to represent the geometrical progression needed to accommodate the actual number of ancestors of any one person.

An Ancestral Chart will contain only names, dates of births, deaths and marriages, and possibly the place of residence of the various people named. It is a skeleton history giving only the vital record.

A Genealogical Chart is a compilation of data with reference to lines of decent. It starts with one common ancestor who may be the emigrant, or one of the emigrants if there were several bearing the same surname, that came to this country in colonial times. Or it may begin with any subsequent ancestor heading a particular branch of the family surname.

For instance, Matthew Cushing with wife, Nazareth, and sons, Daniel, Jeremiah, Matthew and John and Daughter, Deborah, came to America in the ship "Diligent" in 1638.

A genealogy of the Cushing family may include this entire family and their descendants, or it may be the Daniel Cushing genealogy treating only of Daniel, son of Matthew and Nazareth, and his descendants.

Wherever a genealogical time frame starts, it is then brought downward from that point. That downward trail should expound, by generation, the offspring of a chosen forefather.

In other words, if the researcher was compiling the genealogy of his father, (surname), then his other would only be documented to the point of naming her as the wife of his father's children and mother of any children having that father's blood. Birth, death and marriage records should be included. She has no further part in the genealogy of her husband's descending family.

Of the four grandparents the only one with whom he is concerned is the father of his father who bears the same surname, and that grandfather's wife to the same extent to which he carried his father's wife, his own mother, and while all the other grandparents are dropped and ignored, it is the purpose of the genealogy to deal with all the offspring of the one grandfather who is picked up in the blood line of the ancestral name and carry them to some point where it has been determined to drop out those who have changed their surname by marriage.

*"You don't choose your family,
they are God's gift to you."* ~ Desmond Tutu

3 THE HISTORY OF ONE BLOOD LINE

Sometimes the parameters are so strict that the genealogy is restricted to only those persons bearing the same surname as the selected forefather. In that case only the history of sons and unmarried daughters are presented. If preferred, the data may be expanded to include the marriages of daughters and their immediate families.

This is the most common way of presenting a family history and the research style that is usually recommended. If preferred, the descendant line may be expanded to include all descendants of the chosen forefather. This method would then include not only the descendants with the same surname but also include the surnames of the married daughters.

This last method is known as a full genealogy and would be a complete history of all blood descendants from the starting ancestor. This would then present a complete history of one strain of blood.

In summary, an Ancestral History is the history of a descendant (starting point) and his ancestors, whereas a Genealogy is a history of an ancestor (starting point) and his descendants.

Genealogy would include many who are connected by blood ties to the common ancestor, as well as those "brought in" through marriage in the branches. Because of it is of interest to a wider family group, it is often prepared with the intention of publication. The large expense involved in such a publication would most probably be offset by the bigger amount of family members interested in the "Genealogy" report, rather than the more narrow "Ancestral History".

"There are only two lasting bequests we can give our children - one is roots, and the other, wings."
~ Hodding S. Carter

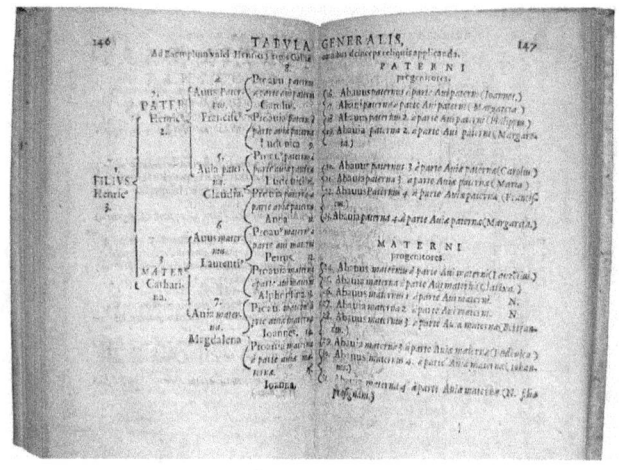

4 KNOW THE NUMBERING SYSTEMS

How To Use Genealogies The Right Way -

Printed genealogies are not always the same. Individual families sometimes prefer more creative ancestry reports rather than the more traditional styles.

If you are lucky enough to acquire a hand printed or published genealogy you will need to learn how to read the numbering system used to create the genealogy.

Listed on the following pages are the most common numbering systems used in the 20th century.

d'-Aboville System -

The d'Aboville System is a descending numbering method developed by Jacques d'Aboville in 1940 that is very similar to the Henry System, widely used in France.

It can be organized either by generation or not.

It differs from the Henry System (next example) in that periods are used to separate the generations and no changes in numbering are needed for families with more than nine children.

See the image on the follow page for an example of this d'Aboville System.

```
1 Progenitor
 1.1 Child
   1.1.1 Grandchild
       1.1.1.1 Great-grandchild
       1.1.1.2 Great-grandchild
   1.1.2 Grandchild
 1.2 Child
   1.2.1 Grandchild
       1.2.1.1 Great-grandchild
       1.2.1.2 Great-grandchild
   1.2.2 Grandchild
       1.2.2.1 Great-grandchild
   1.2.3 Grandchild
   1.2.4 Grandchild
   1.2.5 Grandchild
   1.2.6 Grandchild
   1.2.7 Grandchild
   1.2.8 Grandchild
   1.2.9 Grandchild
   1.2.10 Grandchild
```

Henry System -

The Henry System is a descending system created by Reginald Buchanan Henry for a genealogy of the families of the presidents of the United States that he wrote in 1935.

It can be organized either by generation or not.

The system begins with 1.

The oldest child becomes 11, the next child is 12, and so on.

The oldest child of 11 is 111, the next 112, and so on. The system allows one to derive an ancestor's relationship based on their number.

For example, 621 is the first child of 62, who is the second child of 6, who is the sixth child of 1.

In the Henry System, when there are more than nine children, X is used for the 10th child, A is used for the 11th child, B is used for the 12th child, and so on.

In the Modified Henry System, when there are more than nine children, numbers greater than nine are placed in parentheses. Here is an example:

Henry	Modified Henry
1. Progenitor	1. Progenitor
11. Child	11. Child
111. Grandchild	111. Grandchild
1111. Great-grandchild	1111. Great-grandchild
1112. Great-grandchild	1112. Great-grandchild
112. Grandchild	112. Grandchild
12. Child	12. Child
121. Grandchild	121. Grandchild
1211. Great-grandchild	1211. Great-grandchild
1212. Great-grandchild	1212. Great-grandchild
122. Grandchild	122. Grandchild
1221. Great-grandchild	1221. Great-grandchild
123. Grandchild	123. Grandchild
124. Grandchild	124. Grandchild
125. Grandchild	125. Grandchild
126. Grandchild	126. Grandchild
127. Grandchild	127. Grandchild
128. Grandchild	128. Grandchild
129. Grandchild	129. Grandchild
12X. Grandchild	12(10). Grandchild

NGSQ System -

The NGSQ System gets its name from the National Genealogical Society Quarterly published by the National Genealogical Society headquartered in Arlington, Virginia, which uses the method in its articles.

It is sometimes called the "Record System" or the "Modified Register System" because it derives from the Register System (see below), The most significant difference between the NGSQ and the Register Systems is in the method of numbering for children who are not carried forward into future generations: The NGSQ System assigns a number to every child, whether or not that child is known to have progeny, and the Register System does not. Other differences between the two systems are mostly stylistic.

```
1 Progenitor
  + 2   i  Child
    3   ii  Child (no progeny)
    4   iii Child (no progeny)
  + 5   iv Child
     (–Generation Two–)
2 Child
    6   i  Grandchild (no progeny)
    7   ii Grandchild (no progeny)
5 Child
  + 8   i  Grandchild
     (–Generation Three–)
8 Grandchild
  + 9   i  Great-grandchild
   10   ii Great-grandchild (no progeny)
 + 11   iii Great-grandchild
 + 12   iv Great-grandchild
```

Register System-

The Register System uses both common numerals (1, 2, 3, 4) and Roman numerals (i, ii, iii, iv). The system is organized by generation, i.e., generations are grouped separately.

The system was created in 1870 for use in the New England Historic and Genealogical Register published by the New England Historic Genealogical Society based in Boston, Massachusetts. Register Style, of which the numbering system is part, is one of two major styles used in the U.S. for compiling descending genealogies. (The other being the NGSQ System.)

```
1 Progenitor
    2   i  Child
        ii  Child (no progeny)
        iii  Child (no progeny)
    3   iv  Child
        (–Generation Two–)
2 Child
        i  Grandchild (no progeny)
        ii  Grandchild (no progeny)
3 Child
    4   i  Grandchild
        (–Generation Three–)
4 Grandchild
    5   i  Great-grandchild
        ii  Great-grandchild (no progeny)
    6  iii  Great-grandchild
    7   iv  Great-grandchild
```

Meurgey de Tupigny System -

The Meurgey de Tupigny System is a simple numbering method used for single surname studies and hereditary nobility line studies developed by Jacques Meurgey de Tupigny of the National Archives of France, published in 1953.

Each generation is identified by a Roman numeral (I, II, III, ...), and each child and cousin in the same generation carrying the same surname is identified by an Arabic numeral.

The numbering system usually appears on or in conjunction with a pedigree chart. Here's a simple example of this system.

```
        I Progenitor
         II-1 Child
            III-1 Grandchild
                IV-1  Great-grandchild
                IV-2  Great-grandchild
            III-2 Grandchild
            III-3 Grandchild
            III-4 Grandchild
         II-2 Child
            III-5 Grandchild
                IV-3  Great-grandchild
                IV-4  Great-grandchild
                IV-5  Great-grandchild
            III-6 Grandchild
```

de Villiers/Pama System -

The de Villiers/Pama System gives letters to generations, and then numbers children in birth order.

In this system, b2.c3 is the third child of the second child, and is one of the progenitor's grandchildren.

The de Villiers/Pama system is the standard for genealogical works in South Africa. It was developed in the 19th century by Christoffel Coetzee de Villiers and used in his three volume Geslachtregister der Oude Kaapsche Familien (Genealogies of Old Cape Families).

The system was refined by Dr. Cornelis (Cor) Pama, one of the founding members of the Genealogical Society of South Africa.

```
a Progenitor
    b1 Child
        c1 Grandchild
            d1 Great-grandchild
            d2 Great-grandchild
        c2 Grandchild
        c3 Grandchild
    b2 Child
        c1 Grandchild
            d1 Great-grandchild
            d2 Great-grandchild
            d3 Great-grandchild
        c2 Grandchild
        c3 Grandchild
```

Ahnentafel System -

Ahnentafel, also known as the Eytzinger Method, Sosa Method, and Sosa-Stradonitz Method, allows for the numbering of ancestors beginning with a descendant.

This system allows one to derive an ancestor's number without compiling the list and allows one to derive an ancestor's relationship based on their number.

The number of a person's father is the double of their own number. The number of a person's mother is the double of their own, plus one. For instance, if the number of John Smith is 10, his father is 20, and his mother is 21. The first 15 numbers, identifying individuals in 4 generations, are as follows:

(First Generation)
1 Subject
(Second Generation)
2 Father
3 Mother
(Third Generation)
4 Father's father
5 Father's mother
6 Mother's father
7 Mother's mother
(Fourth Generation)
8 Father's father's father
9 Father's father's mother
10 Father's mother's father
11 Father's mother's mother
12 Mother's father's father
13 Mother's father's mother
14 Mother's mother's father
15 Mother's mother's mother

A perusal through a family index for the person's name closest in line to the person being researched should show the first place in the book where this person is mentioned. There may also be others, but this should be the first "presentation" of that individual where the book will be helpful.

If the searcher does not find that most immediate ancestor, then the search expanded to the next ancestor in line (depending on whether the research is being done in a downward or upward direction).

For example, if the searcher's name is James West, and he knows he is the son of Thomas West and grandson of Samuel West, then he should first look in the index for a Thomas West. The correct Thomas West should be identifiable by dates, marriage etc.

If that is to no avail, then he should expand his search another generation back and search for Samuel West, his grandfather. He should continue searching in this manner until he finds an ancestor that can definitely be identified to the line he is researching.

Now having found a beginning place, the searcher should look at the numbering system used for this "found" ancestor. He should then flip back in the earlier part of the book until he find the same number set out in a list of children. The "found" ancestor's name should appear in this list.

Although there are various numbering or lettering styles found in books, if the system used is not one of the popular ones, then usually there is no explanation on using the system presented. Usually that particular system will not be found again so it has not been presented here because it is not commonly found in practice.

Some of these tracking plans are so complex and odd that it would take a very long time to try and understand each particular process. Often these tracking plans are found to be virtually useless since they are so hard to understand. It is also not time feasible to think you would need to "decipher" each plan of each research book you find, before you could even get into the meat of the data presented. That could potentially add on days and possibly even months to your research project.

Since some of these plans are so detailed and complex, it is entirely possible that the data presented may not be accurate either. With the easier plans, the researcher can easily see whether the numbering or lettering system is correct, because it's is a system that is readily known and used by researchers.

None of the comments here are intended to approve any one method over the other. It just depends on your own personal preference.

"I shall grow old, but never loose life's zest, because the road's last turn will be the best." ~Henry Van Dyke

5 WHERE TO GO? WHAT TO LOOK FOR?

The first questions for someone contemplating ancestral or genealogical research is usually - where do they look and what should they be looking for?

The answers to these questions require some serious thought, because this will be the foundation for your whole project. You could be looking for the RIGHT THINGS, but be in the wrong place. Or you could be in the RIGHT PLACE, but be looking for the wrong things. Either would be a total waste of your time.

Writing your Ancestral History or Genealogy is the simpler part of the project – only a matter of some editorial work. But the hard work is in researching out and then sifting through the data that was found.   If sufficient data is NOT available to begin with, there will be NO finished product. If sufficient data IS available, but you don't know where to find it – there will still be NO finished product. If there is no data, then all the literary and editorial ability in the world cannot produce a family history.

For that reason, what I will be showing you here is of GREAT IMPORTANCE TO A SUCCESSFULLY FINISHED PRODUCT.

When considered as one project, the task seems enormous. But when you break the whole task down into smaller projects, you will soon see it is actually quite a simple plan. Doing only one part of the project at a time is the secret. Then analyze the results from that step to see 1) Is there still enough data to continue? and 2) What is the next step?

Many times multiple family members will decide to take on the combined challenge of creating an ancestral history or gathering a genealogy. But that is really not the most practical way to proceed. The task is better served to have only one leader - only one individual should take up the challenge. That way, multiple parts of the family down-line can usually be worked on at the same time from the same data source. This practice saves both time and expense.

Once the worker finds a new research source, he should devour that source by jumping rapidly from one family line to another since he knows what he is looking for and still needing for the project. That way, with one worker, each new data source is "picked clean" like it's been attacked by a piranha and can then be set aside as already "gone through".

The compiler is not working for public publication, so anything found can be used without question of plagiarism. Often he is able to abstract from a printed genealogy a long line of ancestors for his project. In that situation, his task is merely one of abstraction and arrangement in its proper place in his history or on his chart.

For Ancestral History, it is a simple matter of copying the desired information from books found in Genealogical Libraries. When this has been done, the real work of collecting data begins.

A man finds room in the few square inches
of the face for the traits of all his ancestors.
~Ralph Waldo Emerson

6 Printed Sources of Information

Libraries are always filled with genealogical data that is not available anywhere online. This is particularly true in small towns where private funds have made such information available in small numbers or for a limited publication run. Most small communities do not have the large funding needed to provide such information in a researchable online format. Biographical and genealogical data of varying historical importance have transpired in the history of particular towns or counties.

Their real value as a source of genealogical information may be limited, but it may contain that one small gem of information that your family has been hoping will break down those huge brick walls that have been holding the project back.

Published Town Histories -

There are scores and scores of histories published about specific towns, especially in the New England area of the country. The majority of these town histories are written to document the historical development of a town or community. Often, they will also contain genealogy section about the families which had a part in that early town development.

For example: In the Weymouth Town History, two full volumes are devoted to genealogies.

Typically, these town histories are a fairly thorough look at the early town development and include religious, educational, industrial and civic influences. Men, women and sometimes entire families who have attained prominence in early town affairs are included in town or community histories.

Genealogical sections of these town histories are usually arranged alphabetically and generally begin with events which led up to the "first" family of that town. This will normally include the direct descendants of that early ancestor. These town-history genealogies often cover early residents who spent their entire lives in the town and made significant contributions to the welfare of the town. These usually came in philanthropical or humanitarian, educational or business-development ways. While this research source is important for those dedicated to finding that data on that blood line, it is also limited in effectiveness.

For instance, in the History of Hanover, Massachusetts, on page 389, is found:

William Studley, son of Nathan, married June 10, 1832, Elizabeth C. Haskell, daughter of Jonathan Haskell of Ipswich. They had nine children born in East Abington only TWO of whom we follow.

That particular history then follows along the families of just two of the nine children born into that blood line. Although this helps, it does not help to provide data on the other seven children. In that instance, other research sources must be used to round out the data on this family. Evidently the other seven children did not remain in the Hanover community, so they were not included in that specific "town history".

At that point, it would be wise for the searcher to investigate other towns in Massachusetts. But where should one begin? Back in the same town history the searcher is anticipating discarding.

Hanover says the nine children were born in East Abington. In the Abington History is found a reference to all nine children and in fact the names of all nine children. So although all nine were not fully presented in the Hanover town history, it provided the necessary trail so that when the search viewed the Abington history, the full names were found and can then be further researched. Be cautious not to overlook some critical "clue" when you think you have come to a dead end. It is best to go back and read from the beginning about that which you are seeking – keeping an eye alerted for any small direction to turn next. (such as "were born in East Abington")

Some histories though have never been officially published or the genealogical section may have been eliminated. In that case, the searcher would need to resort to other investigative means to find the data being sought.

Not all New England families are so easily followed in town histories since many have never been printed. They may be handwritten and maintained by perhaps the historical association or some similar organization. In that case, a trip may be in order or the searcher may choose to pay to have a photocopy of the appropriate sections mailed to him.

In cases where family branches have migrated to the central and mid-western sections of the country, it is usually necessary to work from both ends towards a middle connecting the family line. It is best accomplished by running the line in New England until it is lost, then backing up on the various families found in that section of the country to which the migration from the east was supposed to have been made, trusting that a connecting link can be established.

Usually the removals were recent enough that at least one family member remembers the occurrence. Or perhaps they remember hearing an older family member talk about it. Grandmother Brown's Hundred Years is a good example of this.

One word of caution to anyone using town histories for data – be sure to take notice of the date of publication. It's not uncommon for the term "no children" to be noted alongside the record of a husband and wife, or only one or two offspring. The truth may be that couple may have ended up having any number of children.

When this occurs it is often when the publication date shows the history was put together shortly after the husband and wife were married or at least during the first few years of marriage.

The historian should have noted that, as of that time, offspring did not exist. Many of these town histories date back quite far so this is an important caution to bear in mind, assuming, of course, that the searcher intends to be diligent in gathering the correct data.

Another area of caution is in the names of towns and following any name changes through the years. It is not uncommon for some areas of the country to have changed the names of towns through the years. This was evidently quite a common occurrence in Maine. What once was known as Littleborough, Maine, later became known as Leeds. Another similar occurrence the city of Port Royal, which is now known as Livermore.

Many towns and localities and even streets which had been first named for an association to England were often changed after the Revolutionary War. One example - King and Queen Streets in Bristol, Rhode Island, were changed to Constitution and State Streets during this period of time.

Another shock was when certain early settlers were given land grants in Canada. They had packed up their families and made the trip to Canada, only to find the actual land was back in the area they had just left, even though it was stated as a Canada Grant.

Many states often published what was known as a legislative year book or manual. These books recorded any changes in name of towns. By checking with the state in question, or contacting the appropriate Secretary of State or other representatives, access to these books can usually be secured without much difficulty.

Other factors of change to contend with, besides when town names changed, is that some of the larger towns actually divided into separate sections (communities) over time. Each section would then be given a new name and another new town was created.

Sometimes previous town records were carried into the new town records but, often, that was not the case.

Such is the case with Smithfield, Rhode Island. Even though Smithfield is one of the older towns in Rhode Island, the early town records were moved to Central Falls. The Smithfield records were removed in 1895 when Central Falls was set apart from Lincoln. Lincoln had been set off from Smithfield in 1871. Changing locations of town records makes searches more difficult, unless you know the general history of the community. It is always wise to ask for assistance from a resident or the historical society who knows the "old time" changes and development of the area.

State lines have also shifted during the early years of a state's development. One example is the City of Pawtucket, Rhode Island. Pawtucket's early records not only are in a different city but they are in what is now a completely different state, Bristol County, Massachusetts. The old town was part of Rehoboth, Massachusetts, which was later known as Pawrucket, Massachusetts, which later became Pawtucket, Rhode Island. The same shifting can be found in many states. Another example is much of the eastern Tennessee area was original part of Virginia and North Carolina.

Thus when state boundary lines were changed many families were moved from one township or state to another without ever moving from their physical location.

An Extreme Example of State Line Shifts -

John Joles was supposed to have been born, lived and died in Warren, Rhode Island. It was found in records that he died in Bristol, Rhode Island, an adjoining town. This newly found record required that what was believed to be "fact" should now be moved into the "we don't know what happened" column.

Digging for the root cause - it was found that the old Warren-Bristol line passed directly through the Joles house which stood not over half a mile south from the center of Warren village, and that the family bedroom where John slept was on the Bristol side of the line.

The town line was later moved south one mile leaving the entire house a mile on the Warren side. At the time John died, however, if he died in his bed, he was in Bristol. But if he ate in the old-fashioned kitchen, a custom prevailing in the early days, he ate in Warren.

Therefore he doubtless was born and died in Bristol, but lived in Warren all his life, and actually was born, always lived in, and died in the same house and in adjoining rooms.

Another Example of State Line Shifts -

The obituary of a man who recently died in East Providence, Rhode Island, stated that he died in that town, but that he was born in Seekonk, Massachusetts, and followed the statement by saying that he was born in the house in which he died. This was all true.

The record of his birth will be found in Seekonk, Massachusetts, and that of his death in East Providence, Rhode Island, the latter town having been incorporated in 1862 by the settlement of the boundary line between the states of Massachusetts and Rhode Island.

This occurrence was not limited to Massachusetts and Rhode Island, but can be found in all of the eastern states, to one degree or another. These instances show the importance of examining records of adjoining or nearby towns. Some records will make reference to such changes, but many do not. Such details are often omitted from family histories, just because the searchers usually assumed the person had relocated to a neighboring city in their later years. It was often not included in many family histories but just considered assumed the reader would know. When researching town histories, this caution should be kept in mind and histories of nearby communities should automatically be reviewed also. Viewing old maps can also be helpful to more easily see the town changes and restructuring.

Town histories, which are usually considered an excellent genealogical reference, were often prepared quickly for an impending historical anniversary or celebration. In those instances, the histories are not as detailed and precise as we would desire. Often a number of people would work together as a committee to gather the general data, then that work was patched together. Although the end result was intended to be the best it possibly could, time, training and budget restraints often restricted the accuracy of the project. Quite often, many blatant inaccuracies can be found in such compilations.

Published Genealogical Indexes -

It is not uncommon for a searcher to find no published genealogy records for a particular family name and also no formal town history recorded for that area. When this occurs, the journey will be slowed greatly because there is no one profound source he can draw from. He will be forced to gather information from multiple sources and then attempt to assemble the bits and pieces together.

There can usually be found a myriad of sources to draw upon, such as histories, books, genealogies, pamphlets, magazines, etc. These indexes are exceedingly valuable and great time savers. Even if it is a small book, it may be filled with an amazing amount of information.

Sometimes, however, even though there is no formal town history, smaller communities in the area will have gathered their own informal family histories for that particular small area.

These can be profoundly helpful, with family information, cemetery, school, historical photos, all often readily available at a small local "community center", rather than an office building in the larger nearby town. Many times local families have joined to acquire old schools or old churches to prevent them from being razed.

They are then repurposed as a community center for small community gatherings. Attending these community gatherings (usually monthly) is another excellent source of information with some old-timers perhaps even remembering the person or family being researched. At the very least, these real faces will know 1) if there is info available and 2) where it is located.

Oscar Frank Stetson, author of The Art of Ancestry Hunting, published by Stephen Daye Press in 1936, provides the following resource information from his book. After all these years, these sources are still relevant and beneficial. They are presented as follows:

"One of the indexes prepared by Donald Lines Jacobus, M.A., published in 1932 and from which the following example is quoted, illustrates the general character of the work:

"Hawes, Edmund. Duxbury Yarmouth A.i. (65-160) -D. (20-73)

"By consulting the key it is found that the above means that the New England Historical and Genealogical Register (A.i.) volume 65 at page 160, and The Mayflower Descendant (D) volume 20 at page 73 will contain information relating to Edmund Hawes who was in Duxbury and Yarmouth.

"Of the older indexes which are well known and reliable should be mentioned Munsell's List of Titles of Genealogical Articles in American Periodicals and Kindred Works 165 pages, published in 1899, m which information is given in the following form:

"Sherman, Ancestry of Rev. John Sherman and Capt. John Sherman (of Dedham, Mass.) by a descendant of Capt. John Sherman. New England Hist, and Gen. Register L-I (1897) 309-15.

"Another good resource is Derrie's work, published in 1886, also by Munsell. The name of this work is an Alphabetical Index of American Genealogies and Pedigrees and contains 245 pages.

"Both of these are old and of course much has been published to be indexed since they were printed, still they are standard and authentic and by no means should be shunned because of the date of their publication.

"Another good work is Index to American Genealogies and Genealogical Material contained in all Works such as Town Histories, County Histories, Local Histories, Historical Societies, Publications, Biographies, Historical Periodicals and Kindred Works, Alphabetically Arranged. Its information is shown in the following form:

Landon. American Ancestry II 69

Burleigh's Guild Genealogy 96-8

Champian Genealogy 390 New York Gen. and Biog. Rec. XXVIII 24-7 Va.

Mag. of Hist, and Biog. II (1895) Wyman, Hist. Genealogy 116"

"Burleigh's Guild Genealogy 96-8 Champian Genealogy 390 New York Gen. and Biog. Rec. XXVIII 24-7 Va. Mag. of Hist, and Biog. II (1895) Wyman, Hist. Genealogy 116

"For English ancestry, Marshall's Genealogical Guide is recommended. It is also advisable to consult the Catalog of the Library of Congress under the subject of American and English Genealogies."

Published Genealogical Dictionaries -

A Genealogical Dictionary of the First Settlers of New England, Showing Three Generations of that Who Came Before May 1692 is hands down, the most popular, most widely used and the best known in this category. It was prepared by James Savage and was published in four volumes in 1880.

This resource limits each entry to only three generations, the first of which must have been prior to 1692. There are no recent editions since the original was first published in 1860. However, it is thought to be extremely useful due to the authenticity of the data and the specific time period it covers.

The following method, by James Savage and used in his Dictionary, noted above, imparts the following knowledge:

"Bentley, John, Charlestown, perhaps s. of William, d. 20 Nov. 1690. Richard, Charlestown in 1690, had w. Margaret. William, a passenger to Boston 1635 aged 47 in the "True-love," with John, 17, and Alice, 15, perhaps his ch. but where he pich. his tent is unkn. to me, as is also anything a. Mary, a passeng. the same yr. in the "Defence," aged 20. Bentley is a parish in the Deanery of Doncaster and is part of Yorkshire.

"In some families Mr. Savage gives very full consideration as is seen from the abstract of the Breck family as follows:

"Breck, Edward, Dorchester 1636, freem. 11 May 1639, came prob. from Ashton in Co. Devon, was an officer of the town 1642, 5, 6 and after, d. 2 or 6 Nov. 1662. Had Robert wh. he brought from Eng.; John; Mary, Bapt 6 Aug. 1648; Eliz. and Susanna. The w. d. 11 Nov. 1653. His wid. Isabel, who was his 2nd w. and had been bef. wid. of John Rigby of D. m. 14 Nov. 1663 Anthony Fisher; Mary m. 9, Jan. 1687 Samuel Paul; Eliz. m. 11 Mar. 1670, John Minot; and Susanna m. 20 Mar. 1674 or 5 Jonn Harris. But he must have had ano. d. for his will of 30 Oct. 1662, only 3 d. bef. his d. ment. d. Elinor".

As can be seen, Mr. Savage had a unique style with a wide use of abbreviation. This allows a tremendous amount of knowledge to be documented adequately in only four volumes.

There are many resources from which to draw data, however, another dictionary which comes highly recommended is A Genealogical Register of the First Settlers of New England by John Farmer.

It contains alphabetical lists of governors, deputy governors, assistants or counselors, ministers in several colonies from 1620 to 1692.

From 1634 to 1692, it documents representatives of the General Court of Massachusetts during that time, as well as Harvard College graduates to 1662, members of the Ancient and Honorable Artillery Co. to 1662 and also Freemen Admitted to Massachusetts Colony from 1630 to 1662.

Many other Early Inhabitants of New England and Long Island, N. Y. from 1620 to 1675 are included even though they may not fit directly into one of those categories outlined above.

In addition to this unbelievable amount of data already noted, Farmer also added various genealogical and biographical notes collected from "Ancient Records, Manuscripts and Printed Books". The entire work was published in 1829.

This example is taken directly from Mr. Stewart's work, noted above, to show his precise style of treatment:

"Stewart, Duncan. One of the early settlers of Newbury, d. in Rowley in 1717 ae. 100 yrs. Coffin. John, Springfield in 1654 d. 21 Apr. 1690 (See Stuart). Richard, member of ar. co. 1652".

This particular work fits an important niche as it deals only with settlers that can be documented during the period 1620 to 1675. Therefore, it does not matter that it was published in 1829, the book is still the standard to use in researching that particular time frame and location.

Another spectacular index was prepared by Charles Henry Pope and called simply, "The Pioneers of Massachusetts". It is done in much the same style as that of Savage and Farmer. It describes many lists drawn up from the Records of Colonies, Towns and Churches and other Contemporaneous Documents. It was published in 1900 and, with around 500 pages, it is quite a spectacular work.

There is also a very good index for Connecticut that was published by Royal R. Hinman in 1852. It is known as A Catalog of the Names of the Early Puritan Settlers of the Colony of Connecticut, with the Time of their Arrival in the Country and Colony; Their Standing in Society; Place of Residence; Condition of Life; Where from; Business etc. as far as is Found on Record.

Using a similar treatment of data as Hinman in 1852, The Genealogical Dictionary of Rhode Island was published in 1887 by John Osborne Austin and covers old-time Rhode Island families.

Taking a turn to the south, Armstrong's Notable Families comes highly recommended also. The searcher should also check out The Handbook of Genealogy, published by the Genealogical Society of Utah. Although it is prepared by the GS of Utah, it is not limited to Utah and covers much of the occupied states at that time, in so much as data was available to provide.

A searcher should not close out this part of his research before checking with the Genealogical Libraries and Historical Societies. There are many other reliable and useful books on this topic that just what this writer has had time and space to include.

The searcher should always, no matter his source, be certain, to the best of his ability, that the source is considered reliable.

Published Genealogical Magazines -

The New England Historical and Genealogical Register seems the best known of all the old genealogical magazines and books, originally published by the New England Historical and Genealogical Society in Boston. The information contained in this publication is immense, and perhaps most important of all, it has been carefully examined and checked for accuracy as well as indexed extremely carefully.

Next in line in importance is probably the sixty-six volume masterpiece titled the New York Genealogical and Biographical Record. This great effort contains invaluable information.

Also of significant value is a seventy-plus volume of work published by The Essex Institute of Salem, Massachusetts. This large historical and genealogical collection continues to grow with time as it is has been an ongoing project.

There is also the Virginia Magazine and the William and Mary College Quarterlies in the south. Both of these resources are also quite good and well respected.

Here again the writer cautions to always check your resources. There are so many publications of this sort and on this topic, it pays to be judicious in this respect. Some are authentic and valuable but others, as is to be expected, may not be checked as carefully as a searcher would prefer.

It is recommended that before relying on any work the searcher is unsure about, that inquiries be made to reliable historical or genealogical societies in the area to get some idea of its value and authenticity. Even though the work might appear of quality, it is always better to err on the side of caution, particularly with a topic so sensitive and important in nature.

Publications of Hereditary Societies -

The Daughters of the American Revolution – The DAR is one of the best known of organizations known as "hereditary societies". The DAR prints a quarterly publication that tracks the family record of their membership. Due to the strict requirements to join the Daughters of the American Revolution, and proof of family line needed for membership, their data can be pretty well relied on.

While these records may be relied upon, the information conveyed is largely based upon war records of the Revolution and little of general family history will be found other than lines of descent from those who saw service in that war. Still, even that information can be invaluable to tracing family histories.

The Mayflower Society - The quarterly publication of the Mayflower Society is printed under the name of The Mayflower Descendant. Like the Society itself, information is drawn from one group only and that are passengers on the Mayflower only. The publication deals only with them and their descendants.
Like other genealogical magazines and quarterlies, these lesser known hereditary society records should also be deemed reliable. It might still be wise to rely on the recommendation of someone familiar with that particular group.

Published Early Vital Records -

Some states have published either whole or partial copies of the vital records which occurred prior to the point when towns and municipalities were required to record such information.

When these records began depends on what state is in question. Some records date back prior to 1850, such as the records of Massachusetts and Rhode Island. Beginning with 1850, these two states enacted a requirement birth, death and marriage records were to be maintained.

Although there were attempts by several legal and community groups to maintain vital records from the start of the New England settlements, officials often only enforced the law partially or sometimes not even at all.

The New England Historic Genealogical Society, through their Eddy Town Record Fund, made possible the publishing of vital records for the Commonwealth of Massachusetts.

Publications from these historical organizations are given authority over other differing sources because of their documentation requirements. Though there may be variances, all sources should be carefully weighed.

These older historical records can hold no claim to completeness or accuracy as many records were contributed to by family doctors and clergymen – even family headstones. However, there may be many reasons why the records do not justify.

The family doctor may have noted in his dairy the birth of two children in a family.

The minister may have baptized three children of the same family, the name of only one noted being the same as those mentioned by the physician.

The family burial lot may have headstones for a couple more children whose names were not mentioned by either the doctor or the clergyman, and there may have been still others who escaped the physician, baptism and the grave and grew up to rear in their time sizeable families themselves.

These resources with vital statistics will generally give credit to the doctor or minister or note the cemetery and gravestone.

As such there can be no claim as to the correctness of either names or dates. They were often based on a doctor or clergyman who only saw a family once a year or so. There can be a claim for the correctness in copying what was found, but there is no way a copyist could verify whether an original record lacked through either carelessness or misinformation or lack of familiarity to a family they might have seen infrequently.

In the old days journals or diaries were often kept but the writing would probably have been sporadic for one or many reasons. Those who kept diaries during that period were often delayed until later to document an event or entry. By that time, it is possible an incorrect date could have been entered, or possibly even a nickname rather than the given name.

It is not unusual for a minister's diary and that of a doctor could record the same event but on different days. Occasionally a will appear that a will was brought in for probate several days prior to the testator's actual death.

Such events should not alarm or discourage the searcher. Ministers, doctors and town clerks did not often keep their records written on a daily basis but rather, as they had some down time. All mankind is human.

Another important factor to make allowances for is the difference in given name and for nicknames in historical data. This caution has already been mentioned once, but it begs to be presented in more detail. The doctor delivering the baby may have been told the baby would be named Sarah, and he probably entered it into his journal that way. But sometimes parents rethink the naming process (yes, even back in those days) and may have decided to call her Maria after a favorite relative. She may have eventually been baptized as Maria by the family clergy, but the doctor's records would have revealed a female offspring named Sarah.

This is where the detective work must begin. The searcher needs to investigate to decide 1) was it one baby girl with some confusion over the name, 2) was it the same child but with a given name and a nickname, or 3) were twins born to the parents since the birthdates are the same? In research of this detail it's important not to rush through the process of gathering data. A slow and more methodical approach will bring forth a much more accurate record in the end.

James N. Arnold attempted to do for Rhode Island what the New England Historic Genealogical Society did for a part of the Commonwealth of Massachusetts. Such a project entailed speaking with each Rhode Island family to check their family records and the headstone inscriptions. This work would have been an invaluable contribution to the genealogy process. However, the task turned out to be far more involved than Mr. Arnold could have accomplished himself with the care this project deserved. Mr. Arnold's work was published at the expense of the state of Rhode Island, and, although not fully complete, his work still made a valuable contribution to the existing records. Since it did not fully encompass all of Rhode Island, the genealogist using his book as a resource must remember to collect data with an eye towards accuracy of that record and cross-reference that information whenever possible.

Published War Records -

The American Revolution has been notably documented in the seventeen-volume work entitled Soldiers and Sailors of the Revolutionary War. Published by the Commonwealth of Massachusetts, it presents war records of those men who lived in and around that area and who gave their services to the cause for freedom. This information was presented in a neat and orderly fashion and is considered another fine resource.

Sometimes the information is difficult to sift through unless full names were known. But still, the researcher can find more good leads to follow if they will stick with the publication to exhaust all name possibilities. In one example, a search for Joseph Thompson from Massachusetts and who was known to have seen service turns out to be a bit overwhelming. A total of twenty-seven Joseph Thompsons were found and credited for service during that war.

To determine which is correct, more research must be done unless the researcher knows what area of the Commonwealth this particular Joseph Thompson came from.

Few historical books have been published since that time documenting subsequent war records. That is because in later wars, the records of soldiers and sailors were documented in government files and in a more standardized manner. The War and Navy and the Pension Office at Washington can assist with access for wars after the American Revolution.

Published State and County "Gazetteers" -

For the genealogist searching for "sketches of historical importance to a town" will find value in these large volumes. But the researcher looking more specifically for family facts may find them of limited value. These publications were usually privately funded and contain a combination of biographical and genealogical data about a certain town, community, district or county.

Published Court and Land Records -

Several sets of books covering Colonial court and land records, such as the Probate Records of Essex County Massachusetts, have been published and distributed to libraries through the years. Suffolk Deeds is a set of more than a dozen volumes covering early land transaction in Suffolk County in Massachusetts.

If a genealogist can wade through these old records, they will find an abundance of rich information and can be of great importance and convenience to the researcher. It is often possible that the searcher can view them in a nearby library, rather than travel to Salem or Boston, Massachusetts to examine the originals.

The searcher may be able to find what he wants in transcripts and then, if desired, he can contact Salem or Boston libraries for a better copy of the originals, if needed. No time or money is wasted in the search unless the searcher decides to travel to Massachusetts himself.

Published Biographical Sketches -

This is fascinating if you have ancestors from an area of the country where Biographical Sketches were published. These books usually had beautiful elaborate covers and were filled with actual steel engravings or "photogravures". They were often titled Representative Men of Vermont or Encyclopedia of Biography.

For a family to have been included, a private subscription must have been purchased by the family.

Then biographical sketches of those persons and their immediate families would have been added. If the amount of the subscription was large enough, a photograph or "photogravure" would have been included as well.

A biography would have been written by either the subject himself or his view of himself and his family, or was prepared by an editor from material furnished by the subject.

Unfortunately, the "Representative Men" was all too frequently only about those who had deep enough pockets to afford the subscription price rather than the real characters who played a substantial role in forming their town. Too often important biographies of "real" community role models were omitted because they had no "financial interest" in the work.

Although these works are interesting if your ancestor in question may have been financially well established during those years, they do not follow actual blood lines and are by no means a true family history.

It should also be noted that these works rarely provided the full truth of a family but rather the truth as the participating family who paid the subscription wanted to be printed.

Published Books of Heraldry -

Heraldry and coats of arms is important enough topic or a book all its own, and there are many good works on the subject. But for the purposes of this book, it will be only touched upon here. It is the intent of this writer to provide information on a few standard works that the normal researcher may not know about. Hopefully, this work will give the reader a few new resources to delve into deeper. Some may choose to hire an expert on "heraldry" if they wish to find their true family coat of arms.

But here are a few works that good libraries will have in their genealogical department.

Dictionary of the Peerage and Baronetage of the British Empire by John Burke Genealogical and

Heraldic History of the Landed Gentry in Great Britain and Ireland (3 volumes) by Sir Bernard Burke

Vermont" America Heraldica (author unknown)

A Registry of American Families Entitled to Coats of Armor from the Earliest to the Present Time by Crozier

For Students - Introduction to Heraldry by Clarke and the Complete Guide to Heraldry by Fox Davies.

Published English Records -

Various sorts of English records are presented in many books. Their primary emphasis is the Court, Church, Parish and various other records and lists. They are considered valuable for the research to consult.

The individual books have not been listed here as the information contained in them is so varied. I recommend that when a researcher gets to this point in his ancestry (English ancestry) that he consult with a local librarian who may be able to suggest the best work this particularly library has for further information.

"Enjoy the LITTLE things in life, for one day, you may look back and realize they were the BIG things. ~Robert Brault

7 Original Information Sources

The searcher is encouraged to seek out any unpublished documents which may also be of extreme benefit to his research. Bibles, diaries, journals, cemetery records, deeds, wills and land records are all original sources of information that must be sought after with relentless zeal.

Every searcher for family history will be tremendously amazed by the number of families in his family tree that have information to consider. Some have saved information for sentimental reasons – others for biographical reasons. Regardless, if the searcher will contact family members that are still living, he may find a treasure trove of data already gathered to further his cause.

The researcher who walks into a large genealogical library feeling he has scored a huge find may also find disappointment as he realizes the search must continue to the record offices of larger cities. There he will find scores of orderly files and indexes to sort through which is always a painstaking task, regardless of experience. His route will also take him to small towns that may have no order at all to their records. Also in his future, he will probably find dusting off ivy-covered cemetery headstones to find inscriptions grown hard to read with time and perhaps even in to private homes to view a dusty family Bible pulled from a hope chest or attic hideaway in hopes of reading faded entries of long ago.

The searcher will find two things that occur. First, published books will often provide masses of material in a short time, whereas delving into unpublished records will become a dreadfully slow task.

Being a good genealogist is neither easy nor fast. Many projects take years and years to complete. It is not a task for one that is easily discouraged. It is easy to copy information readily available but quite another to travel miles and miles to new towns and dig for days over boring and hard to read records searching for a single birth, death or marriage records.

Thank goodness for telephones and email. Often the two modern conveniences can make the process simpler if the searcher happens to find a helpful and friendly voice and attitude on the other end. Sometimes the person on the other end can find what you need quickly, either for free or a reasonable charge. Even when there is a charge, it may be cheaper than what the researcher would spend in time and travel costs to dig through piles of unfamiliar books.

Original Vital Records -

A letter, phone call or email to the Secretary of State in question will give the genealogist the appropriate state office to provide what data is desired. Now all states are required to maintain vital records. But some states begin keeping such records before it was mandatory. So the history of vital records may date back farther than others, depending on when record keeping began in that particular state.

In some instances, data from town clerks, diaries of clergy and doctors, from church book, cemeteries and family bibles have not yet been published. If that is the case, then it becomes the researcher's duty visit the necessary libraries and state offices to search out whatever original documents are available

In fact, it may become necessary to do to anyway, if the published records contain such error as to the point where the data cannot be reconciled. It is certainly possible that errors in vital records can also occur as they are being recorded by human hand entering the data.

Be aware that if the researcher desires to search the actual original record, arrangements may need to be made ahead of time. In larger cities, much of that data is on actual microfilm or data disk now. But make sure to clarify the availability of the data before a trip is wasted. Also, some smaller town offices are only open certain days and times of the week.

It's hard to imagine in this day and age but it is possible that in some towns records may be kept in non-climate-controlled buildings. If that should be the case, then all the more reason to make arrangements ahead of time so the appropriate record books can be moved to a climate controlled location where conditions will permit the work being done.

If arrangements are not made in advance, it is conceivable the researcher will be told to come back another day to allow time for the books to be found and gathered. Not only would that delay be discouraging but could increase the travel costs with an extra day of lodging and food. It is always better to check ahead and find out exactly what the situation is for the town you are visiting.

The same applies from "Published Vital Records" as it does for Original Vital Records. Omissions and errors are abundant in these types of records for any number of reasons. Even worse, nothing at all can be done about it. Usually, land and court records are fairly correct. But in vital statistics and diaries, the data was often entered quickly, without supervision, and probably without question or need for verifying the data. It all boils down to the data being what the recorder chooses to enter or leave out.

Quite often family differences or disputes are often found to have crept into record keeping.

Here is one such instance, as related in "The Art of Ancestry Hunting":

"On the occasion of looking up the heirs of a man who died several years ago, there was found one living child. The examiner was told that there was one son who died in infancy. The records showed the birth of a John and, soon after, the death of a Richard – aged only a few weeks.

Was John living? If so, something was wrong with the dates. Upon consultation with the mother, the examiner was told, "I wanted to name the baby John and his father wanted to name him Richard, but we named him John". It is interesting to read between the lines. Mother had her way, but Father got in the last word, even if it did complicate the records".

Early vital statistics recording, before it actually became mandatory, often contained errors. However, if the researcher finds the data to give no reason for doubt when compared to other information already obtained, then it is reasonable for the researcher to take it as good.

If, however, something does not reconcile or stands out as conflicting, then it behooves the researcher to throw up the red flag and do more research. Enough research should be done until the genealogist can say the information he presents is as near correct as possible.

Original Probate Court and Land Records -

It is always a good idea to run a search through Probate Courts and Land Records just in case there is some gem awaiting there for the researcher. A good genealogist never assumes there is nothing of value in a resource, especially one as important as Court and Land Records. After all, with all the work the researcher is already doing, it is a small issue to check one more source as well.

Wills are always important sources, as they usually list children of the testator by name and also give the name of the surviving wife or husband. Wills will often list other family members if the deceased died without children.

Land records too can be valuable because they will usually furnish the given name of the wife or husband. When the seller is a married person, in some states the husband or wife must sign off their courtesy or dower rights in order to convey a clean title.

The discovery of an unfamiliar name will sometimes reveal a second marriage which had not been found from other sources.

Equity Court records can also be helpful if the courts had divided any land.

In the case of early settlers, checking early court records is also a good idea. These early court records can usually be found in the state archives.

It is wise to check with the Capital or State House to ascertain exactly where they stored records and how to access them. Consulting early state history, early census records and old muster rolls can be exceedingly helpful.

Original Family Bibles -

In early times, the universal custom of keeping records in the Family Bible was an honored task. This source is always the first preferred source of reliability. A father and mother, better than anyone else, would surely know the intimate matters as their family birth dates, the date of their marriage, and the dates of the births, marriages and deaths of their children.

There is an instance where a Rhode Island town clerk entered a child's birthdate as July 9th, 1772. However, after the child was grown and bore sons of his own, their respective family bibles indicated their father, Benjamin, was born on July 31st, 1772.

There is little doubt that these two sons would know their father's birth date better than a town clerk.

It is not known whether the town clerk made the mistake or someone giving him the information gave him the wrong date. Regardless, based on how hard travel was in 1772 and how long it took get word spread from one place to another, it is amazing the birth even got recorded. It is believed that this recorded birth (though wrong) was one of only two that were recorded out of a large family of children.

As researchers we must all remember the people attempting to record this type of information for future generations were trying their best and perhaps we can be somewhat charitable with our criticisms. It is a wonder that we who search are able to find so much historical records and any discovery of an old family Bible should be considered as gold.

Cemetery Records -

As far as correctness goes, gravestones should have been considered next after the family Bible in reliability. However, most people place gravestones after vital records. The reasoning is that due to the high cost of stone engraving, an error made by the engraver was rarely corrected.

Sometimes errors on tombstones were intentional, as this example shows:

Underneath this pile of stones Lies all that is left of Sally Jones. Her name was Lord, it was not Jones, But Jones was used to rhyme with stones.
Here's an example of intentional ambiguity, as this Massachusetts stone shows:

(Name Left Blank) was somebody, who, is no business of yours.

Incorrect dates on grave stones frequently occur. Stone markers were often erected much later after a death occurred. By that time, the one who ordered the stone may have been unsure of the precise date of death after so much time has passed.

Still gravestones were helpful for information in early times. The gravestones usually gave the month, day and year of birth and death, if known. Later it became more common to only give the year of birth and year of death. This could give an incorrect age by nearly two years depending on whether the birth or death occurred in January or December of the respective years.

Besides the explicit dates of birth and death, a gravestone often offered other information as well. A stone marker in New York also bore the minister's name who gave the funeral service and the biblical reference used in the funeral message.

To most, this information is not considered valuable as far as genealogy research goes. Another stone, this one in a Massachusetts cemetery, is unique in that it had a small niche cut in the marble. The niche was intended to protect a small tintype photograph of the deceased. The tintype was protected by an ingenious marble cover hinged in such a way that it protected the picture from the elements but could swing open to reveal the photograph inside.

At times, gravestones have even become a method of advertising, albeit somewhat disrespectful to the deceased, as shown in this example:

Here lies Jane Smith, wife of Thomas Smith, Marble cutter. This monument was erected by her husband as a tribute to her memory and a specimen of his handiwork. Monuments of this style are two hundred and fifty dollars.

Experienced genealogists will recommend anyone conducting such research should, whenever possible, examine actual family burial plots. It will aid the researcher in locking in birth and death dates but may also reveal other family members of which no record at all was found.

In the Benson Family Record (published) is a list of the family of David and Jane (Seymour) Benson in which are the names and dates of ten children. These were found on the various records relating to the family. In the family burial lot, however, are stones for "Son David" and "Daughter Jane."

In no other place are these children mentioned and were it not for a search of the cemetery there would be no knowledge of these two children who evidently died in infancy. They were a part of the family and should be included in any genealogy recording the children of their father and mother.

By examination of the birth dates of the recorded ten children it will be found that between the fourth and fifth and between the eighth and ninth children as listed there was a much longer period than between any other births, and it was in those places probably that these two children came in the family.

This is not unusual for many years ago, it was quite common for children to die in their youth, be it from lack of nearby medical treatment or from some physical accident around the homestead.

The Original Source - The Family -

In an Ancestral History many different families are under consideration in order to make up the whole finished work. Few of these individuals will have the same interest with the searcher but all should still be willing to participate toward the finished work if they are able. A yearbook published by the Institute of American Genealogy of Chicago called The Handbook of American Genealogy, includes an alphabetically arranged list under the caption of "Genealogies in Course of Construction." A great many ideas to follow can be found in a little used resource like this.

Besides a personal conversation with family members, the next course of action is to write letters (or email) to potential family historians/genealogists.

The letter may be phrased something like the following:

To or Dear _____,

In preparing genealogical records of the _____Family, I am seeking information of the ancestors and descendants of the persons indicated below.

I note you are interested in families bearing the same surname. I would appreciate any assistance you may be able to render or any suggestions as to a source of information which will help me in following out this line. I shall be glad to reciprocate with any matter which I may have in my files.

Sincerely yours,

————

(address)

(city/State/Zip)

(date)

This same form letter can be used for genealogical work to secure information of the families of daughters who have married into other surnames, if it is desired to include them in a full genealogy.

Corresponding with private individuals is more important when there is less information available, whether online or offline. Finding and getting in touch with various family members is an important task for the genealogist.

Unless the members of a family are found and data is secured from them, then there can be no real genealogy done. That information must be sought out and found from every corner of the country, if needed. When finished, it is possible even small genealogies may index up to ten thousand names. That means information must be obtained from a great many people concerning many individual families in the down-line if a good genealogical structure is to be built.

A good genealogist is like an architect designing a great structure and visualizing the completed structure even before ground is broken. Great builders realize that the greatest structures are built by placing one stone upon another from the deepest foundation to the pinnacle capstone.

In addition to a personal chat with individuals, the visit should include a look at any Family Bibles. Often people forget they have one tucked away somewhere. It is important to ask if the individual inherited one or knows who does have one in the family.

The Family Bible may be stored in great-grandfather's trunk in the attic and has not been taken out in years, simply because people don't think of it often. If there is one, it is recommended the interviewer ask for a copy of its entries if it seems to be of value in the search. There may also be other Family Bibles, containing important family records, in other branches of the family. It is wise to also ask if the person being interviewed knows of other Family Bibles. If the interviewer doesn't think to ask, no one may think to share that information with him and valuable data could be lost.

It is also a good idea to "send out a plea", either by a phone call, letter or email, telling family members what the researcher is doing and that he would now like to examine any Family Bibles that might still be around. They should all be hunted down and examined for missing pieces of the genealogical puzzle as well as verification on what information he has already gleaned during his search.

Normally these Family Bibles will be in the possession of the older family members as maintaining a big Family Bible is not as popular of a tradition in recent years as it was years, and generations, ago.

The person being interviewed should be invited to revisit any old memories that pop into their memory – happy or sad, serious or funny. The interviewer should not intend to be brief in his visit. Once old memories begin to start returning, encourage the person to ramble from thought to thought if that is how their mind is working. Invite them to share any history or tradition or family tale they may have had stored in their minds for years. You can take time later to sift through the "tales" for relevancy.

Be sure to get specific name and locations while you are taking notes. The interviewer must ask for those type specifics. Otherwise, the person may not think to share or even think of where it happened or where they lived then.

The writer of a genealogy now in process of construction recently said that as a child he had a hazy remembrance of hearing his grandmother tell of cousins in a western New York town. No other member of the family remembered anything of them or their place of residence, but investigation found people of the same name in that town who had lost the line of where they belonged in the family.

The grandmother's remark of many years ago seemed to be suggestive as a key to the whole situation. The names of these cousins were not remembered, but the name of the town, one word, was associated with the grandmother in memory and it is apparently enough to connect two large branches of the family.

Records should be made of the names of every person or place mentioned regardless of whether it is known at the time when and where they are going to be used, or whether or not they will even be used at all.

There is perhaps no period in the development of the family from early settlements to the present generation which is as elusive as that age just prior to the memory of those living at the present time.

Early history is fairly well known because of old documentation that is available, and memory will reach back for roughly three generations without trouble. But the intervening period of time, that joins the early and the recent years, is the one that proves to cause the most trouble.

Any family search should also include any manuscripts that might be available. Nearly every family has had one or more family members who, at some time or other, have been interested in ancestry. They may have even attempted to write some part of the family history.

Perhaps they only jotted down some items, intending to organize and publish it at a later date. Chances are, they may have set it aside and just never reached the writing out period. Usually the researcher is told to check with

"Aunt Emma" or an "Uncle John", who once started to write the history of his immediate family.

Such notes will probably be found written in pencil, perhaps even on multiple odd-sized sheets of paper. Certainly not a dignified job of gathering data, but perhaps, it will still be of some help to the present researcher. If several people in the family have attempted this task in the past, make every possible attempt to gather and piece together the information.

Any local historical or genealogical society should be visited, and the same done in any area where the family resided for significant time. The catalogues of these societies may have fragmentary histories that can be beneficial to the project. These societies often have old photos that can photo copied. Even if the society has nothing noted on the family in question, ask to see photos pertaining to the appropriate time frame or locality. For example, if the interviewer knows his grandfather owned a barbershop during the early years of town he can ask about photos of barbershops. Even though the barber's name may have gone unrecorded, still there may be a photo of the shop in the society's files. Others in the family may well recognize his grandfather, perhaps even someone else in the photo as well.

Papers and old photos of this sort, found after death and which no one in the family cares to keep, are often given to a local historical society. There they are usually placed in an envelope, properly catalogued, and filed for reference.

Sometimes the person who did the gathering of the material, realizes it is not enough for publication but too valuable to toss out. Or the person may realize there is not enough family interest to take on the task to its full extent

It is both interesting and sad that there are often quite complete compilations that are given to a society because there were not fund available for publication at that time. Many of these are found written neatly and protected in notebook form. Many represent years and years of painstaking work by the compiler. If the researcher fails to check the historical society, he may never find some of the most valuable of material, including historical photographs.

So, now that the researcher is to this point, what happens next? If he wants to reach the largest number of family members, he will need to make some lists. Up to now, he has primarily been working on the Ancestral History or preparing a Genealogy alone.

In ancestral work he will continue to do so, but in genealogical projects the time has arrived when he must cease making independent examinations, copying his own findings and conducting the entire project as a lone worker.

Now is the time to ask for help – he must enlist help from all corners of the country or globe where any living relatives reside. Now the researcher changes hats from compiler to editor, as he prepares to join his work with that of others in the family.

This should now become a family-wide project, and every effort should be made to reach every living family member bearing the surname and any down-line the search has revealed. Enlist their help to make sure the researcher has everyone noted.

The genealogist should ask family member to go through any directories, address books or email lists for family connections in their area of the country.

This method builds up a great mailing (or emailing) list and will save time in the future. Plus it is necessary if the researcher's message or request is to be conveyed correctly to everyone of the extended down-lines. If the researcher relies on someone to ask someone, who will then pass the request on to someone else – well the message will never be conveyed exactly right.

Besides the researcher should make sure all members have his mailing address and direct contact information. If some family member are retired or have extra time on their hands, their help could be enlisted as needed. They will enjoy being part of such an important project to their family. Small errors anyone might make now are not critical since this is not part of the final work.

Now is the point where questionnaires can be mailed out to furnish names and addresses and any other pertinent information. The questionnaires are specifically looking for male family members bearing the surname being researched. Female lines will also be secured, along with any information regard marriage and offspring that will bear a different surname.

In sending out questionnaires it is advisable that upon the return of the questionnaire, each reply is checked against the mailing list already gathered. If each one is taken and checked as received, it is a much easier task that if the researcher waits until they all come back to begin the cross-checking process.   At that point, it could become an overwhelming work

"The real voyage of discovery consists not in the seeking new landscapes but in having new eyes." ~ *Marcel Proust*

8 WHO AND WHAT TO ASK?

Other Written Information Sources -

Besides connecting with family members, the researcher should also visit depositories in search of the originals. Both of these steps have already been discussed. In this section, forms to make the task simpler will be addressed.

Beyond researching official published records kept by municipalities, the genealogist often must go to various depositories and search the originals. As already suggested, be certain to coordinate with the offices in question about times and locations for access to their records.

Be prepared for omissions and errors in original records. In land and court records, entries were usually correct. But in vital statistics and diaries, information was often entered without supervision. Entries could have been subject to the whims of what the recorder chose to enter or omit.

From Family - Asking For Written Information -

Information must now be sought from many people if the process of preparing this genealogy is to be successful. Obviously, it would be a daunting task to write individual personal letters to each family member. So, it is justified in this situation to mail or email a questionnaire or form.

Contacting potential family member can result in a delightful correspondence but the reply might contain only minimal pertinent information. That is why specific questions are a necessary evil.

To get definite answers, definite questions must be asked. But it is suggested that great care be taken in designing the questions so the recipient does not feel like it is an intrusion. You must also respect their privacy, while still desiring to receive important information.

Sometimes questionnaires frighten people. They may become reluctant to participate. People who freely write pages and pages in letter format may shy away from "filling in the blanks", particularly if it asks personal or embarrassing questions, like date of birth.

The genealogist should be assured that there is no "perfect" form that every recipient will understand and be pleased to receive. No matter how carefully the questions are worded or arranged, some will be "put off" or confused by it. So the best case scenario is to write the best questionnaire the researcher can and then accept that not every recipient will participate or return it. That is just the way it is.

Here are some tips that should help design the questionnaire. It should be simple, clear to read and understand, and as short as possible. It should cover all the necessary points but contain no unnecessary words. If explanations or instructions are necessary, make them clear enough that there is no room for misunderstanding or misinterpretation of them. Still, the less wording on the form – the better it will be. It is also wise to leave plenty of room to answer all questions.

Most people have knowledge of at least two generations back from themselves (3 generations). So it is advisable to send the questionnaire in a form that allows room for three, or possibly even four, generations can be gathered. Yes, this will bring in duplicate information, but that just gives more opportunity for the genealogist to verify against errors.

Here is one example of a suitable form – Here we are assuming that the genealogist is to write the history of the descendants of William Curtis who came to New England in the "Lion" in 1632. The form letter could go something like this:

Dear Cousin:—

I am gathering genealogical information on the descendants of William Curtis who came to New England in the ship "Lion" in 1632. He was in Boston that year and in Roxbury in 1633.

I'm asking family members to help with this project. If you could, please fill out the enclosed form and return to me at the address noted below, as soon as possible.

Yes, there are four sheets enclosed. But I've tried to make this as easy as possible for everyone. The first sheet is for you and your own family and your name should be at the top. The second sheet is for the family of your parent in the Curtis line and the parent's name should be at the top. Information on that part of the family should go on this second page.

The third sheet is for the family of your grandparent on the Curtis side and that grandparent's name should be at the top, with the family information on the form.

Please give full names whenever you can, rather than partial names or family nicknames. Any other information or questions can go under "Notes". Then I can follow up on that section when I receive the form back. I have included a fourth sheet should you happen to be able to go back further than the three generations noted. I, of course, would appreciate any other names and addresses you might have of descendants of William Curtis.

I know this will take up some of your time, but please give all the assistance you can. It will benefit all of us in the family.

Sincerely,

Charles G. Curtis (your name)

Please address all communications to:

Charles G. Curtis

10 Main Street, (your name and address; also include your email address if you wish)

Jamesville, Mass.

The form pages should be identical and stapled so they remain in the appropriate order.

Another good psychological tip is to number the papers. (not the pages, the papers) A better response will probably come if people realized their form is being tracked with a number. People feel more careful about returning numbered papers.

The numbers should be based on "sets", not individual pages. Once the set is returned, if the fourth page has not been used, then go ahead and discard it.

If the researcher has found a legitimate family coat of arms during his research, it is wise to use it as a "logo" on the correspondence page and the questionnaire pages. Although heraldry is not traditionally recognized in America, there are still many people who respect their heritage and a coat of arms represents that heritage and tradition. Using a coat of arms judiciously should wake some family members up and cause some excitement for the project. This will come in handy since you are asking family members for help on the project and should encourage cooperation and assistance.

From Public Officials - Asking For Written Information -

Although most public officials are more than happy to help with genealogical work, when possible, consider their side a well. It is not fair to ask for a great deal of assistance without offering to pay an appropriate charge for their assistance.

Staff members, clerks, registrars and court officials are busy with their regular responsibilities. If providing an unusual amount of assistance for personal genealogical research may very well take them away from their regularly appointed tasks. A thoughtless genealogist might sometimes ask for a assistance that would take one or several days of an employee's time. So it is reasonable to expect to pay some reasonably fee, particularly is copies of records are being provided to the genealogist.

It is fair to ask if the name sought appears in the birth, marriage or death records or in the indexes of the land or probate records. That type research can usually be done quite quickly, just enough to confirm the seeker is in the right place. It is wise for the researcher to provide as much information as possible, such as an event to reference or perhaps a time frame. That assures the staff member can get the job done with the least amount of time wasted.

Once the clerk can confirm there is information on file, it is reasonable for the genealogist to make his own trip to the site to review and abstract information he is interested in.

In his inability to do these things, he should write to the clerk and ask the cost of having someone in his office make the examination for a fee. This shows consideration for the staff and municipality office. If the service and fee is agreeable to both parties, then the searcher should forward his payment by mail with a detailed and clear request for information. This will avoid the question of financial responsibility and the clerk can readily make the proper refund if too much has been sent or render his bill for the additional work above the estimate given.

From Librarians, Historical or Genealogical Societies –
Asking For Written Information -

Many people assume that one of the duties of a Curator
or Librarian of a Historical or Genealogical Society is to
furnish genealogical information to all those seeking it
and to give instruction to those who wish to enter upon
the project of building up a Family History or a
Genealogy.

Such is not the case. Providing those personal services
are not part of the curator's or librarian's duties. His
responsibility is to guard the books and manuscripts
entrusted to his care carefully. Included in that care is
responsibly renting or lending them to such persons
who, by membership or otherwise, are entitled to their
use. He is to also see they are given good care and
properly returned unharmed to their place in the library
after having been used, and generally to have the
oversight and care of the library.

Since he is knowledgeable about what is stored, where
and how, in the library or historical society, he may be
able to provide valuable help to patrons of the library.
A good librarian is also willing to accommodate
reasonable requests and offer appropriate advice when
possible when someone appeals to him for assistance.
That does not mean he can accept a task that will
interfere with his regular duties though.

Once he has made the decision whether the task is too
entailed to undertake and still conduct his appointed
tasks, his opinion must be respected by the inquirer.
He is not a teacher of genealogical research, nor is he
meant to examine document and verify specific facts or

data. However, he may choose to undertake some tasks outside of his regular hours of work, and anyone seeking that extra service should cheerfully expect to compensate him for his time and expertise.

A quote on this point from a little handbook put out by the genealogical department of the Public Library of the City of Los Angeles, CA, will express the position of every librarian:

"The library does not compile genealogies. Every effort is made to assist patrons making use of the books and material in the Library, or to direct inquirers to outside sources of information. But the actual examination of records and taking of notes must be done by the compiler of the genealogy".

There are always definite rules of courtesy which must be followed, as well as rules for certain government offices and/or storage libraries. The best results will come when the searcher makes every attempt to cause the least trouble to the office or staff in question and be as respectful as possible for their normal tasks and operational practices.

"A good genealogy is a treasure, and a poor one is often an abomination."
~ Oscar Frank Stetson

9 Conclusion

In entering upon so important an undertaking, there are several points definitely to be determined at the very outset. The genealogist is going to delve into matters private and public; valuable and inconsequential. He is going to become a collector and an editor. He is to deal with human events in their most intimate character—the family life—and reveal them to the eyes of the world.

These events will be intensely interesting to him, and the success of his work will depend upon his ability to portray faithfully these events, coupled with family vital records, in such a manner as to make them reliable sources of information, as well as interesting and profitable both to members of the family and others who have occasion to consult his work.

First, last and all the time he must strive to make his record accurate. Its usefulness depends almost entirely on this element. Genealogy is a statistical record, and as such should always be borne in mind by the writer.

No one expects to read such a record as literature, but he does expect to consult it for facts, and that expectation must be met and satisfied by the faithful genealogist.

This point cannot be too strongly emphasized. All statements must be true in a genealogy, or the reason given for the belief that they are true.

A book of statistics of a family is no place to record guesses and suppositions, nor is it a place to evade indisputable facts.

The utmost caution should be exercised to get and give correct dates and spellings. Though they may be pronounced alike, Smythe is never Smith or Smyth in the written record and the genealogist must enter exactly what he finds, with no variations.

If he finds variations, either in dates or spellings, he must enter his authority for each and put them all in the record that he is preparing.

One line can be followed from a common ancestor. If there were in the emigrant family seven children who grew to maturity and had families, all of those families can be picked up in the father and worked down, or the family of any one of the seven children may be run and the others left alone. If only one line is run well, it is a valuable contribution to history. Rather than to begin too discouraging a work, it is suggested that only one line be attempted at a time.

It must always be borne in mind that the pursuit of genealogical knowledge may be made as simple, or as complex, as the researcher desires. The task will be made more enjoyable if there is passion and some family connection in the project. But, even when the task is taken on as a job for another family, human interest and the curiosity for all things historical are the only necessary ingredients.

Customers who purchased Dig Up Your Hidden Family History might also be interested in:

Yuma Mesa Homesteaders 1948 And 1952
by
Debra Trigg Conrad

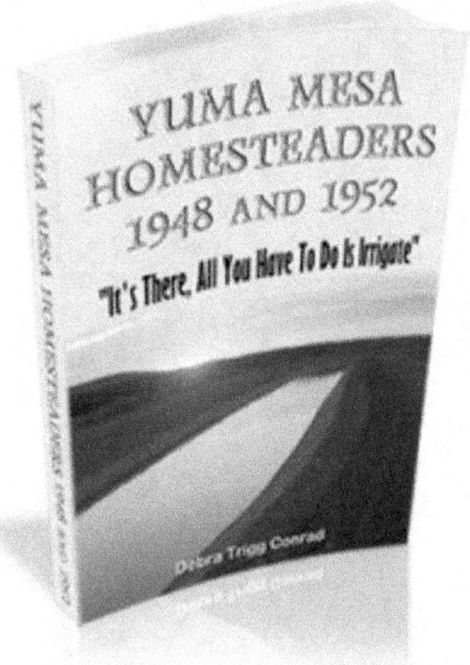

Imagine – Living Without Electricity or Plumbing!

"Find Out How Some of These Homesteaders Fought The Local Electric Company and the United States Government and - WON!"

The Yuma Mesa Homesteads were only a short 7 or 8 miles from Town, but they lived in rural and primitive conditions – some for years!

Though many original homesteader stories are lost forever, this in-depth history is both a testament and a legacy to those who follow today, with its colorful patchwork of precious first-hand accounts.

Spanning the events of "real life", from heartbreaking to humorous, the homesteader stories and photos gleaned from a gathering of Yuma Mesa Homestead survivors is a fascinating read.

Anyone who values the rich historical perspective of rural life will agree; don't let their history be forgotten.

Between these covers is a timeless message for all of us.

From homesteader grandchildren, to rural life historians and genealogists…

let the voices of the past speak to you today.

"Hi, this is Debra Conrad, author of Yuma Mesa Homesteaders 1948 and 1952.

"This has been a supreme adventure and a labor of love. The Yuma Mesa Homemakers Club formed a book committee years ago so all the Homesteader Families could have a format to leave a legacy for their families.

Fullerton Man Wins Farm in Yuma Project

Austin Lempke of 521 Princeton Circle East is one of the 27 veterans who will receive farms in the Gila division of the Yuma Irrigation Project ranging from 113 to 160 acres.

There were applications from 4,111 veterans in every state and all the territories. Names were drawn Tuesday to determine winners of the land which is mostly undeveloped, but is served by new canal extensions which bring in Colorado River water.

"This group had been through three authors and countless frustrations, and then we found each other.

"This project had already had a rocky start when the Yuma Historical Society asked me to take over this effort.

"Many flukes and a good amount of fate brought us together ,and this book is the joyous result.

"But I <u>am</u> someone who dearly loves her hometown, and I wanted to see 'All' of Yuma's unique history preserved – no matter how long or how much effort it took to accomplish the end result.

"You have to realize that I still don't think I 'really' wrote this book. This book seemed to write itself.

"You see, every story was told in each homesteaders own words.

"All the photos are the families' own originals. About 1/2 of this book is filled with documents, newspaper articles and magazine articles gathered after countless hours at the Yuma County Library and also going through Arizona archives online.

"This book is a tiny bit of Yuma history that I hope will give the reader a hint of the fortitude and passion the Yuma Mesa Homesteaders must have had in those early days.

"If you love the west and are even slightly curious about western history, I promise you'll find these personal stories fascinating! I know I certainly did!"

YUMA MESA HOMESTEADERS 1948 and 1952
by
Debra Trigg Conrad

www.yumamesahomesteaders.com/

www.ingramcontent.com/pod-product-compliance
Lightning Source LLC
Chambersburg PA
CBHW070205290526
45789CB00002B/919